ADDISON-WESLEY

DESTINATIONS IN SCIENCE

Authors
David C. Brummett
Karen K. Lind
Charles R. Barman
Michael A. DiSpezio
Karen L. Ostlund

Contributing Authors
Jim Hopkins
Vallie W. Guthrie
Michael B. Leyden
Gerry M. Madrazo, Jr.
Sheryl A. Mercier
Jerome M. Shaw

Activity Consultant
Doug Herridge

Addison-Wesley Publishing Company
Menlo Park, California ▪ Reading, Massachusetts ▪ New York ▪ Don Mills, Ontario ▪ Wokingham, England ▪ Amsterdam
Bonn ▪ Paris ▪ Milan ▪ Madrid ▪ Sydney ▪ Singapore ▪ Tokyo ▪ Seoul ▪ Taipei ▪ Mexico City ▪ San Juan

Destinations in Science™ is a trademark of Addison-Wesley Publishing Company, Inc.

Contents

Unit A
Senses and Health

PICNIC

Unit B
Animals and Plants

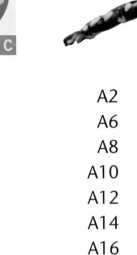

POND

Unit C
Matter

Unit D
Pushes and Pulls

CARNIVAL

Unit F
Weather and Seasons

BEACH

Unit E
Rocks, Sand, Soil

CONSTRUCTION SITE

DESTINATIONS IN SCIENCE

Unit F Beach: 6BL E. R. Degginger; 6BR Peter Miller/The Image Bank; 6T David Young-Wolff/PhotoEdit; 8B Tim Ryan/Gamma Liaison; 8TL Don Hebert/FPG; 8TR Dale E. Boyer/Photo Researchers; 10BL Willard Clay/FPG; 10BR L. West/FPG; 10TL Dennis Hallinan/FPG; 10TR Amy Etra/PhotoEdit; 22(inset) Peter Bennett/Viesti Associates, Inc.; 22–23(background) David R. Frazier Photolibrary; 23B P.L.I./Viesti Associates, Inc.; 23C Photo ESA; 23T Mark C. Burnett/Photo Researchers; 24 Dennis Hallinan/FPG.

Lillian Gee* 1L, 7BR, 9, 12, 13, 17, 19
Michael Groen* 1R, 7TL, 11, 15

*Photographed expressly for Addison-Wesley Publishing Company, Inc.

Illustrations

Unit A Picnic: Doron Ben-Ami 6–7, 10–11, 14, 18, 20–21; Susan Johnston Carlson 7T, 9C, 11B, 13B, 15T, 17L, 19B, 21B; Patrick Chapin 2, 3, 4, 5; Louis Pappas/Pronto 7C, 9R, 11T, 13T, 15B, 17R, 19T, 21T; Jane McCreary 7B, 17B; Josie Yee 8–9.

Unit B Pond: Anthony Bloch 2, 4, 5 titles; Susan Johnston Carlson 16–17 border; Ebet Dudley 14; Doug Henry 20–21; Jane McCreary 9BR, 19TL; Louis Pappas 7T, 9BL, 11T, 12T, 15T, 16T, 19TR, 20; Rodica Prato 2–3, 4, 5; Yin Ling Wong/Pronto 7B, 9T, 11B, 12B, 15B, 16B, 19B.

Unit C Grocery Store: Jane McCreary 7B, 19B; Louis Pappas/Pronto 9B, 11T, 13T, 14B, 17B, 18C, 18–19 border, 20B; Ed Parker 2, 3, 4, 5; Andrea Tachiera 7T, 9T, 11B, 13B, 14T, 17T, 18T, 20T; Josie Yee 12, 16–17.

Unit D Carnival: Chi Chung 2, 3, 4, 5; Louis Pappas/Pronto 7, 9, 11, 13T, 15, 16, 18, 21; Jane McCreary 13B, 19; Nancy Tobin 6, 8, 10, 12, 14, 20.

Unit E Construction Site: Lloyd Birmingham 7T, 8T, 11B, 13B, 15B, 17T, 18T, 21T; Greg Harris 16–17; Doug Henry 6–7, 12, 14–15, 20–21; Paul Meisel 2, 3, 4, 5; Jane McCreary 9, 18B; Louis Pappas/Pronto 7B, 8B, 11T, 13T, 15T, 17C, 18C, 21B.

Unit F Beach: Ebet Dudley 7T, 9T, 11T, 13C, 15B, 17B, 19T, 21BL; Jennifer Hewitson 6, 8, 10, 12T; Barbara Higgins-Bond 14–15, 16–17, 18–19, 20–21; Jane McCreary 11B, 21BR; Mas Miyamato 2, 3, 4, 5; Louis Pappas/Pronto 7B, 9B, 11C, 13T, 15T, 17T, 19B, 21T; Josie Yee 12–13B.

Design

TWINC: Interior design format and design implementation

Literature

Unit A Picnic:
"The Teddy Bears Picnic." Words by Jimmy Kennedy. Music by John W. Bratton. Copyright © 1947 Warner Bros. Inc., renewed. All Rights Reserved. Used by permission.

Unit B Pond: Haiku (Frog) by Basho from Basho et al., Japanese Haiku, translated by Peter Beilenson (Mount Vernon, NY: Peter Pauper Press, 1955, 1956). Copyright © 1955, 1956 by The Peter Pauper Press, renewed.

Haiku (Dragonfly) by Chisoku. Japan, 17th Century. Translation by R. H. Blyth.

Haiku (Nightingale) "Unconventional Debut" by Kikaku from A Net of Fireflies, translated by Harold Stewart (Tokyo, Japan: Charles E. Tuttle Co., Inc., 1960). Copyright © 1960 by Charles E. Tuttle Co.

Unit C Grocery Store: Rachel Field, "General Store" from Rachel Field, Taxis and Toadstools. Copyright © 1926 by Rachel Field, renewed 1953. Used by permission of Doubleday, a division of Bantam Doubleday Dell Publishing Group, Inc.

Unit E Construction Site: From Byrd Baylor, Everybody Needs a Rock. (New York: Charles Scribner's Sons, 1974). Text copyright © 1974 by Byrd Baylor. Reprinted with the permission of Charles Scribner's Sons, an imprint of Macmillan Publishing Company.

Unit F Beach: From Mary Serfozo, Rain Talk. (New York: Margaret K. McElderry Books, 1990). Text copyright © 1990 by Mary Serfozo. Reprinted with the permission of Margaret K. McElderry Books, an imprint of Macmillan Publishing Company.

PICNIC

Senses and Health

PICNIC

Contents

The Teddy Bears' Picnic

by Jimmy Kennedy

If you go down in the woods today,
you're sure of a big surprise.

If you go down in the woods today,
you'd better go in disguise.

For ev'ry bear that ever there was
will gather there for certain, because
today's the day the teddy bears
have their picnic.

Ev'ry teddy bear who's been good
is sure of a treat today.

There's lots of marvelous
things to eat,
and wonderful games to play.

Beneath the trees where nobody sees,
they'll hide and seek as long
as they please
'Cause that's the way the teddy bears
have their picnic.

Eye Spy!

What can your eyes tell you?
What do you see in the picture?
Tell about what you see.

MUSTARD

HOT DOGS

A 6

PICNIC • Senses and Health • Lesson 1

What's in the Basket?

You will need

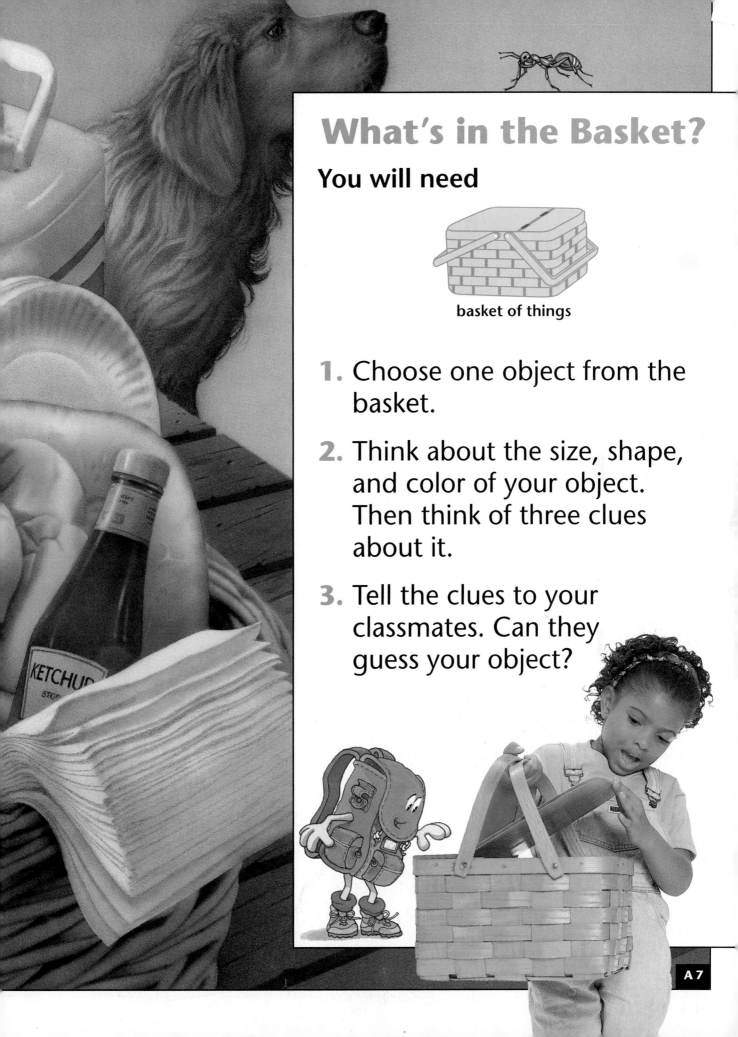

basket of things

1. Choose one object from the basket.

2. Think about the size, shape, and color of your object. Then think of three clues about it.

3. Tell the clues to your classmates. Can they guess your object?

All Eyes On Us

What can your eyes tell
you about people?
Look at the pictures.
How are the people alike?
How are they different?
Who is happy?
Who is sad?
How do the others feel?

Make a "Faces Show Feelings" Book

You will need

camera or crayons   paper   stapler

1. Make a face that shows a feeling.

2. Have your partner draw your face or take your picture.

3. Have your partner make a face that shows a feeling.

4. Draw your partner's face or take a picture.

5. Staple all the pictures together to make a class book.

Now Hear This!

What can your ears tell you?
Look at the picture.
What do you see that
makes sounds?
Tell about the sounds.

Shake, Listen, and Guess

You will need

crayons · small cartons · recording sheet

Activity Journal 3

1. Shake the cartons. Listen carefully.

2. Which cartons sound the same? Color the cartons on your paper.

3. What do you think is inside? Write or draw your guess.

4. Now look inside. What did you find? What clues did you hear to help you make your guess?

How Does It Sound?

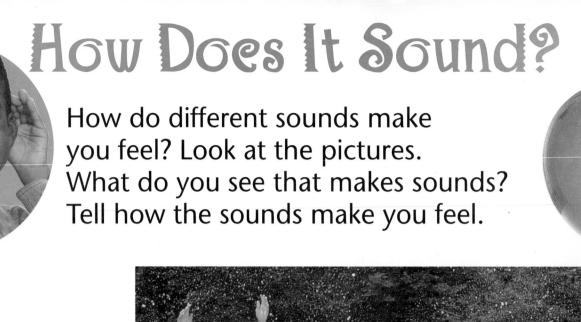

How do different sounds make
you feel? Look at the pictures.
What do you see that makes sounds?
Tell how the sounds make you feel.

Find out how your classmates feel about different sounds.

Take a Sounds and Feelings Survey

You will need

crayon   recording sheet

Activity Journal 4

1. Name a sound. Write the name on your paper.

2. Ask your friends how the sound makes them feel.

3. Color a 🙂 if the sound makes them feel good. Color a ☹ if the sound makes them feel bad.

4. What did you find out about your sound?

What Smells!

What can your nose tell you?
Look at the picture.
What do you see that has a smell?
Which smells do you like?

Sniff and Guess

You will need

1 2 3 4 5 6

small cartons

Activity Journal 5

recording sheet

1. Sniff the cartons.

2. Which ones do not have a smell? Write the numbers.

3. Which ones do have a smell? Write the numbers.

4. Guess what is inside the cartons that smell. Write or draw your guess.

5. Now look inside. What did you find? What clues helped you make your guess?

At Your Fingertips

What can you find out when you touch things?
Look at the pictures.
Tell how each thing feels when you touch it.

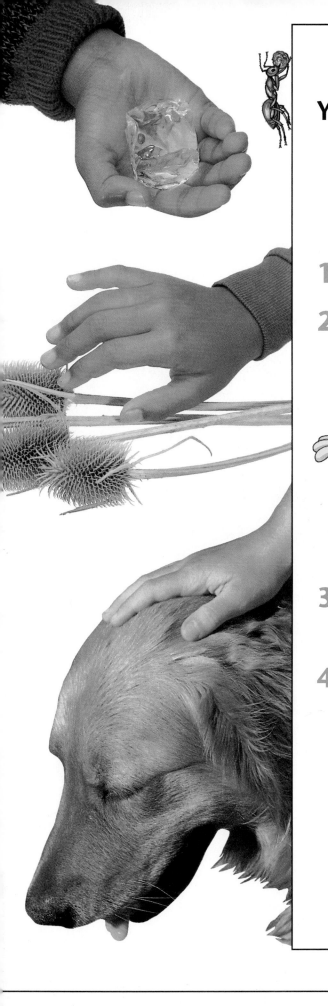

Touch and Tell

You will need

bag of things

1. Close your eyes.
2. Feel in the bag.

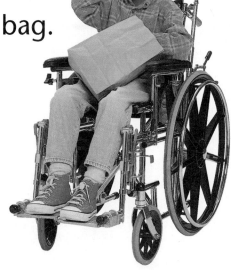

3. Choose two things that feel alike. Tell how they feel.

4. Can you guess what they are?

Yum, Yum!

What can you find out when you taste things?
What can you tell about the foods in the picture?
What tastes do you like?

Taste Test

You will need

pieces of apple   pieces of potato   blindfold   cup of water

1. Put on a blindfold. Have your partner get two kinds of food.

2. Have your partner give you one kind, then the other. Can you tell what foods you tasted?

3. Take a sip of water.

4. Now hold your nose and repeat step 2.

5. Trade jobs and do the test again.

To Your Good Health

How can you stay healthy?

Washing Away Dirt

You will need

dirty strips   water   soap and water

1. Predict which will get cleaner:

- the dirty strip washed in
- the dirty strip washed in

2. Wash one dirty strip in .
Rinse it out.

3. Wash one dirty strip in .
Rinse it out.
Which got cleaner?

Meet a Teacher!

My name is Joel Goldfan. I teach students who do not hear well. I always look at the person when I am speaking. This way students can see my mouth and read my lips. I use a lot of pictures when I teach. Pictures help my students learn more about what I am saying.

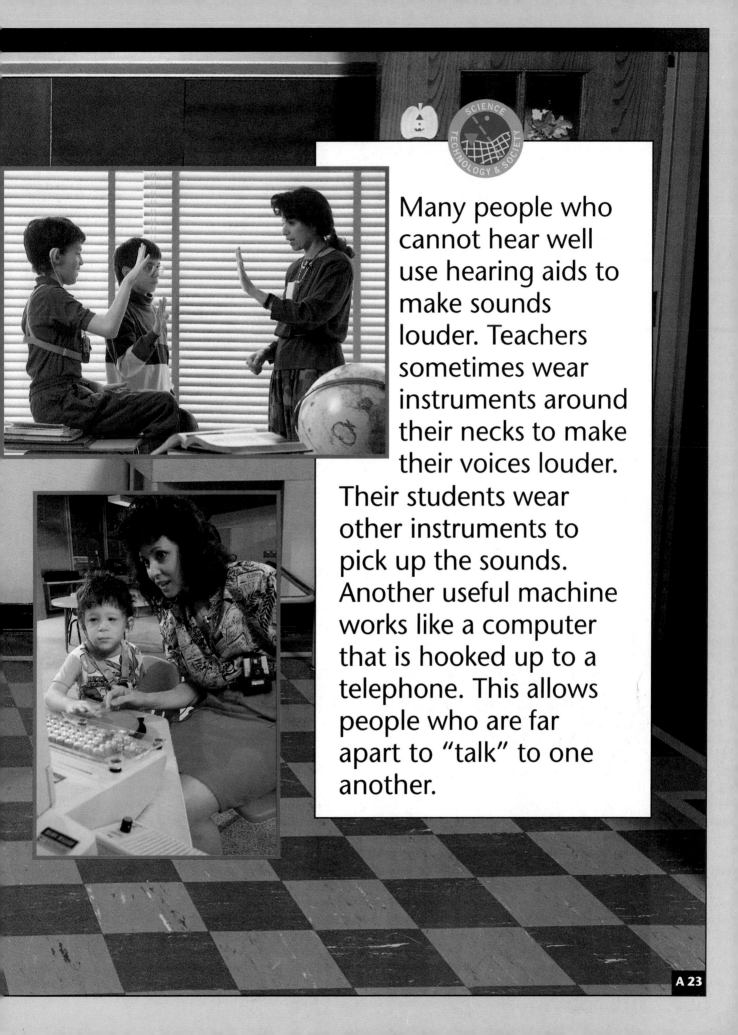

Many people who cannot hear well use hearing aids to make sounds louder. Teachers sometimes wear instruments around their necks to make their voices louder. Their students wear other instruments to pick up the sounds. Another useful machine works like a computer that is hooked up to a telephone. This allows people who are far apart to "talk" to one another.

Glossary

feel *page A16*
To find out by touching.

feeling *page A9*
An emotion, such as joy, anger, or fear.

smell *page A14*
An odor.

sound *page A10*
What is or can be heard.

taste *page A18*
The flavor of something that you eat or drink.

touch *page A16*
To put skin on or against something.

POND

Animals and Plants

POND

Contents

DRAGONFLY

Chisoku

The face of the dragonfly

Is practically nothing

But eyes.

FROG

Bashō

Old dark sleepy pool...
Quick unexpected frog
Goes plop!
Watersplash!

NIGHTINGALE

Kikaku

The little nightingale
Of buff and brown
Singing its first song—
Upside down!

On the Move

Fish **swim**.

Turtles **walk**.

Snakes *crawl*.

Frogs **JUMP**.

Birds *fly*.

Make an Animal Mask

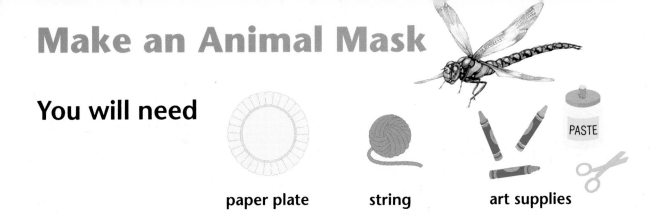

You will need

paper plate   string   art supplies

1. Choose an animal to make.

2. Get a paper plate with eyeholes cut out.

3. Add ears.

4. Add a mouth.

5. Add a nose or beak.

6. Put on your mask...

and Move Like the Animal!

Cover Ups

Body coverings help animals stay warm and dry. Body coverings also help keep animals safe. What kind of body covering does the rabbit have?

Fur keeps a fox warm and dry.

Scales help keep a snake waterproof.

The shell protects a turtle from heat, cold, and danger.

Feathers keep a bird warm and dry and help it fly.

B 8

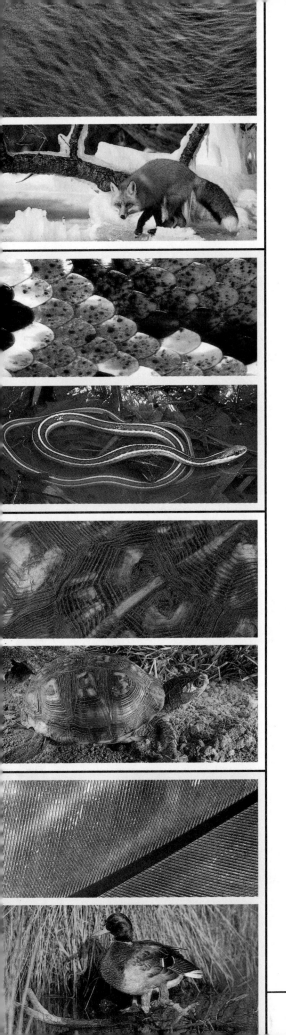

There are reasons why animals are different colors. How does color help the animals pictured here?

Hide and Seek

You will need

colored paper

paper shapes
in different colors

1. Take a large piece of colored paper.
   What color is it?

2. Put some different colored shapes on the paper.

3. Which colored shapes are easy to see?
   Which colored shapes are hard to see?
   Tell why.

Beastie Bites

Beaks

Beaks help birds get food. Each type of beak has a special job.

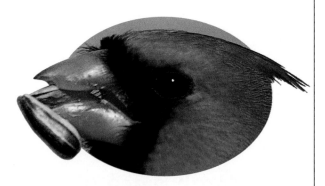

strong beak for cracking

long beak for reaching

long, pointed beak for spearing

Teeth

Animals have different kinds of teeth. Each kind has a special job.

flat teeth for grinding

strong teeth for cracking

sharp teeth for biting

Mouths and Tongues

Animals have different kinds of mouths and tongues. These help them get and eat food.

tongue for catching

strong mouth for biting

long tongue for sensing odors

How Does a Goldfish Eat?

You will need

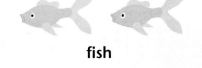

fish food   fishbowl

fish

1. Place a small amount of food in the bowl.

2. Watch how the fish eats.

3. Tell about what you see.

How Do You Eat?

B 11

Lots of Leaves

Leaves come in many sizes, shapes, and colors. Notice how leaves are different.

Silver Maple

Make a Leaf Rubbing

You will need

leaves

paper

crayons

Quaking Aspen

1. Choose a leaf.

2. Put it between two pieces of paper.

Weeping Willow

Dogwood

Sugar Maple

Bigtooth Aspen

Maidenhair Fern

3. Hold the papers down with one hand.
Use a crayon to rub over the leaf.

4. Tell about your leaf rubbing.
Compare it with others.

Poplar

Sycamore

Sassafras

Apple

Norway
Maple

Staghorn
Sumac

Oak

B 13

Plant Parts

Plants need air, water, and light.
Each part of the plant helps the plant get
what it needs.

The stem holds
the leaves up to
get the sunlight.
The stem also
carries water to
the leaves.

Leaves use sunlight
to make the food
the plant needs.

Roots take in
water from
the soil.

How Plants Get Water

You will need

cup of water

RED
red food coloring

paper towel

white daisy

Activity Journal 17
recording sheet

1. Put a small amount of water in the cup. Add red food coloring.

2. Put a paper towel in the cup. What happened?

3. Put more water and food coloring in the cup.

4. Put the flower in the cup. Look at the flower the next day.

Draw what happened.

B 15

Super Seeds

How Seeds Grow

You will need

beans

cup

soil

plastic bag

paper strips

Activity Journal 19   Activity Journal 20

2 recording sheets

Cattail

1. Put soil into a cup.
Add some water.

Butterfly Weed

Wild Pansy

2. Place 2 beans in the cup. Push the beans to the side. Cover the cup with a bag.

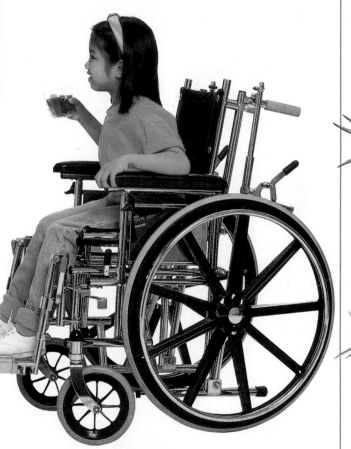

3. Put the cup in a warm, light place. Keep the soil damp.

4. Look at your plant every day. Draw and write about what you see. Paste paper strips to show how your plant grows.

Arrow
Arum

Sedge

Silver Maple

B 17

Is It Alive?

It makes its own food. It grows and changes. It can't move from place to place. **What is it?**

It needs food. It moves in the water. It decides where to go. **What is it?**

It moves from place to place. It needs something to make it go. It can't think or feel. **What is it?**

It moves in the wind. It doesn't eat. It doesn't mind if you walk on it. **What is it?**

It always falls down. It can be round or flat. It can't decide where to go. **What is it?**

How to Play
Pond Squares

1. Read the riddle.

2. Find the picture that answers the riddle.

3. Tell if it is living or nonliving.

Make up more riddles.
Work with a partner.

Make up a riddle for .

Make up a riddle for .

Make up riddles for other living and nonliving things. See if your classmates can guess the answers.

It moves in the air. It eats bugs. It decides where to go. **What is it?**

It lives out doors. It has 4 legs.

Pond Neighbors

Many plants and animals live at the pond.

What's at the Pond?

1. Pick something in the pond picture.

2. Use what you have learned to answer these questions.
   - Is it living or nonliving?
   - Is it a plant or animal?
   - Why do you think it is at the pond?

Meet a Ranger!

I am Jill Johnson. I work in a national park in Alaska. In winter, part of my job is to patrol the park on a dog sled. I make new trails in the snow. I also check on the animals. In summer, I talk to visitors about the dogs and show people how they are hooked up to sleds.

Many different animals live in parks. Sometimes animals are hurt. Sometimes mother animals cannot care for their young. Rangers help care for these animals until they can live on their own.

Glossary

animal *page B7*
A living thing that moves from place to place and finds its food.

body covering *page B8*
The outside part of an animal.

leaf *page B12*
A green part of a plant, usually thin and flat, that grows on a stem or up from the roots.

living *page B19*
Being alive.

nonliving *page B19*
That which is not alive.

plant *page B14*
A living thing that makes its own food and does not move from place to place.

root *page B14*
The part of a plant that grows down into the soil.

seed *page B16*
The part of a plant that can grow into a new plant.

stem *page B14*
The part of a plant that holds the leaves and flowers.

GROCERY STORE

Matter

GROCERY
STORE

Contents

GENERAL STORE

By Rachel Field

Someday I'm going to have—a store!
With a tinkly bell hung over the door,
with real glass cases and counters wide,
and drawers all spilly with things inside.

There'll be a little of everything:
bolts of calico, balls of string,
jars of peppermint, tins of tea,
pots, and kettles, and crockery.

Seeds in packets, scissors bright,
kegs of sugar, brown and white.
Sarsaparilla for picnic lunches,
bananas and rubber boots in bunches.

I'll fix the window and dust each shelf,
and take the money in all myself.
It will be my store and I will say,
"What can I do for you today?"

Here, There, and Everywhere!

Matter is here, there, and everywhere.
In fact, everything in the world is matter.
Matter takes up space. Matter can be measured.
Matter can be any size, shape, or color.
Sometimes you may not be able to see it at all!

What's in the Bag?

1. Watch as your teacher takes each item out of the bag. Tell about its size, shape, color, and how it feels.

2. Tell about two items in the bag. Which one takes up more space? Which is heavier?

3. What can you tell about all the items in the grocery bag?

What's the Matter Here?

Name the matter you see in this grocery store.

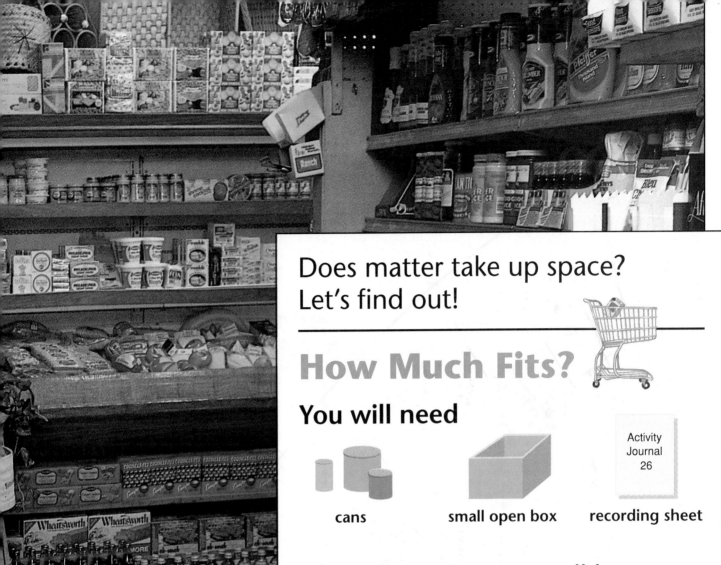

Does matter take up space?
Let's find out!

How Much Fits?

You will need

cans   small open box   recording sheet

Activity
Journal
26

1. Put a can into a small box. Put another can into the box. Does it fit?

2. If it does not fit, tell why. If it does fit, put in more cans until one does not fit. Why doesn't it fit?

Sizing It Up

What can you learn by measuring matter? Let's find out!

You can measure how tall, long, or wide something is.

You can measure how much space something takes up.

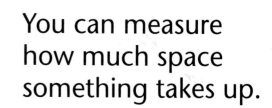

C 10

Measuring Matter

You will need

grocery items

large box of rice

cups

paper clips

recording sheet

1. Make a chain of paper clips. Hold it next to the box.

2. Count the paper clips. How tall is the box? Record what you measure.

3. Pour the rice into cups.

4. Count the cups. How many cups of rice are in the box? Record what you measure.

 Now measure other grocery items.

Matter in My World

Everything in the world is matter.
Matter can be solid, liquid, or gas.

Make a Class Matter Chart

You will need

butcher paper

crayons

grocery items

Activity
Journal
33

recording
sheet

1. Put the paper on the floor.

Solid

2. Write the words **Solid, Liquid, Gas** at the top of the paper. Draw lines to make a chart.

3. Get some grocery store items. Put them where they belong on the chart.

4. Tell about the things on the chart.

5. Now make your own chart about solids, liquids, and gases.

Liquid

Gas

Meet a Cashier!

My name is Joanne Garcia. I am a cashier in a grocery store. I weigh the fruits and vegetables on a scale. I tell shoppers how much they have to pay. The shoppers give me money and I give them change.

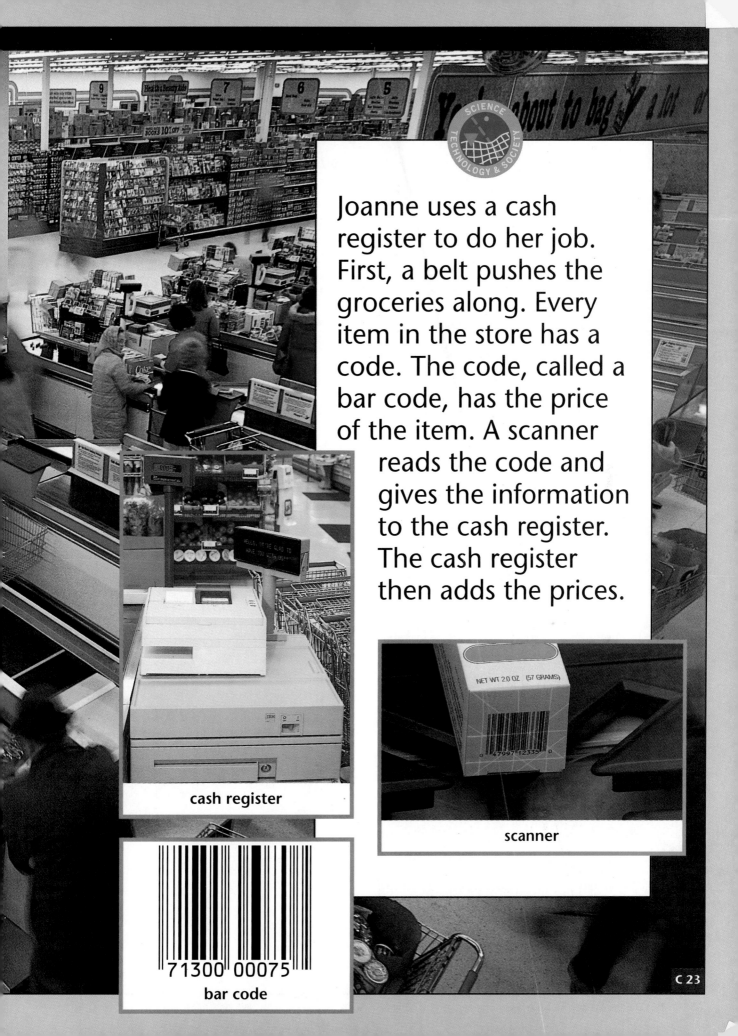

Joanne uses a cash register to do her job. First, a belt pushes the groceries along. Every item in the store has a code. The code, called a bar code, has the price of the item. A scanner reads the code and gives the information to the cash register. The cash register then adds the prices.

cash register

scanner

71300 00075
bar code

Glossary

bubble *page C16*
A thin film of liquid that is round in shape and filled with air or other gas.

gas *page C16*
Matter that has no shape or size of its own.

liquid *page C15*
Matter that takes up space and takes the shape of the container it is in.

matter *page C6*
What everything in the world is made of.

measure *page C6*
To find the size or amount of.

solid *page C15*
Matter that does not change shape when it is moved.

CARNIVAL

Pushes and Pulls

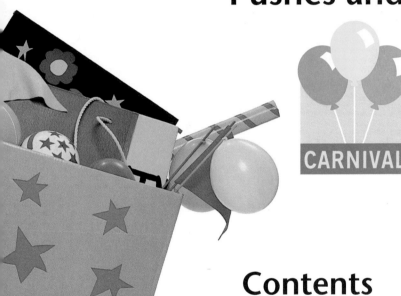

Contents

The Fair

by Myka-Lynne Sokoloff

I went to a fair,
my school fun fair.
I had twenty pennies
jingling in my pocket.

RING TOSS

Portraits by Ben

I would spend my pennies
at the school fun fair,
the twenty pennies
jingling in my pocket.

What would I do?
What would I buy
with the twenty pennies
jingling in my pocket?

There were rides to take
and games to try
with the twenty pennies
jingling in my pocket.

I could bounce a ball
or toss a ring on a peg,
catch a fish in a pool,
or eat something cool
with the twenty pennies
jingling in my pocket.

Ned said, "See how fast you can hammer in a nail with the twenty pennies jingling in your pocket."

That looked like fun, but it wasn't the one way to spend the twenty pennies jingling in my pocket.

I wanted something neat, something I could keep for the twenty pennies jingling in my pocket.

BEAN TOSS

FROG RACE

Well, I had a good day
because I finally found a way
to spend the twenty pennies
jingling in my pocket.

I bought a fish I could keep in a dish.
I went home from the fair with a smile on my face
and a goldfish in a jar in my pocket!

Get a
Fish !

Start with Pushes and Pulls

A carnival is coming!
Everyone helps to get things ready.

The boy pulls a wagon.

The girls push
a big box.

Pushes and pulls make things move.
Pushes and pulls are called forces.

How Can You Make It Move?

You will need

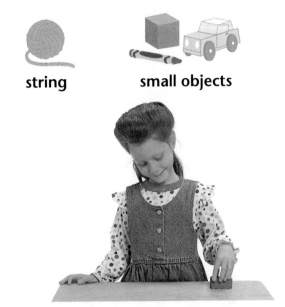

straw   tube   string   small objects

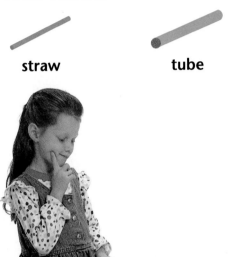

1. Choose an object. Put it on your desk. Is it moving?

2. Use your hand. Make the object move.

3. Try again. Use your hand a different way to make the object move.

4. Now use a tube, a string, or a straw. What other ways can you think of to make the object move?

Stop with Pushes and Pulls

Pushes and pulls can start something moving.
Pushes and pulls can also stop something that is moving.

Rocket Ride

You can make a game called Stop and Go to find out more about these forces.

Playing Stop and Go

You will need

shoe box   signs   recording sheet

Activity Journal 37

1. One child will show the signs.

2. When you see the GO sign, make the box move. Did you push or pull?

3. When you see the STOP sign, make the box stop moving. Did you push or pull?

4. Write what you did on your paper.

Moving Every Which Way

What can pushes and pulls do?

Make things move.

Make things stop.

Make things go slower or faster.

Make things change direction.

Amazing Maze

You will need

blocks   table-tennis ball   straws

1. Use blocks to build a maze.

2. Put the ball at one end of the maze.

3. Blow through the straw. Make the ball move, stop, change speed, and change direction.

4. Move your ball through your amazing maze! Then move it back the other way.

Going with Gravity

Each of the juggler's balls goes up.

Then each ball comes d$_o$$_w$$_n$.

A force called gravity pulls the balls down.

Gravity pulls things toward the center of the earth. Without gravity, everything would float!

Penny Drop

You will need

chart paper

5 cups

5 pennies

chair

Activity Journal 41

recording sheet

1. Draw a big star. Put the cups on the star.

2. Kneel on the chair. Drop each penny. Try to get one coin in each cup.

3. Count the coins. Color your paper to show how many coins you got in the cups.

4. Talk about what makes the coins fall.

Moving with Magnets

At this booth, everyone plays a game called Away We Go.

AWAY We GO

The boy is holding a magnet. A magnet can pull some metal things to it. The force of a magnet can also push another magnet.

Learn more about what a magnet can do by playing this game.

Away We Go

You will need

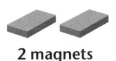

2 magnets

art supplies

Activity Journal 42

pattern

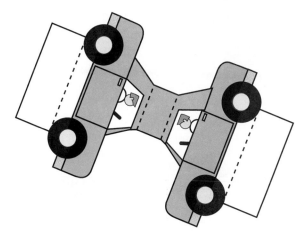

1. Color and cut out a car.

2. Fold the car along the dotted lines.

3. Tape the bottom flaps together. This will make the car stand up.

4. Put a magnet inside the car. It will fit in the bottom.

5. Use another magnet. First pull the car. Then push it. Talk about what you did to change a pull to a push.

Making Static

Static electricity is another force. It can push or pull things. You can make static electricity by rubbing things together. Find out how.

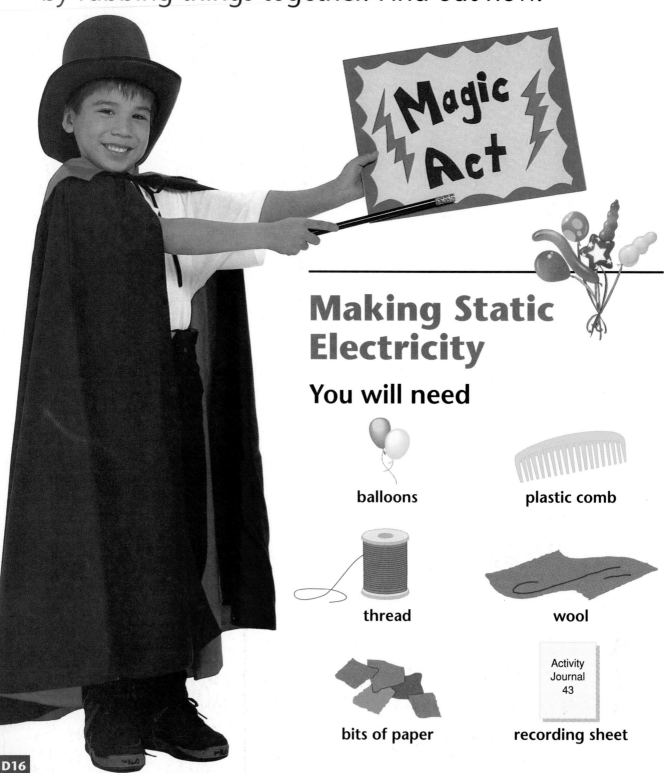

Magic Act

Making Static Electricity

You will need

balloons

plastic comb

thread

wool

bits of paper

Activity Journal 43

recording sheet

1. Rub a balloon on your hair. Hold it near the wall. Draw what happens.

2. Tie thread to two balloons. Rub each balloon on your hair. Hold the thread in the middle. Draw what happens.

3. Rub a comb with wool. Hold the comb near a piece of thread. Draw what happens.

4. Rub a comb with wool. Hold the comb over bits of paper. Draw what happens.

Marvelous Machines

A machine is something that helps you do work. A machine makes work easier.

Here's a carnival treat that's easy to make and fun to eat! What machines do you use to make it?

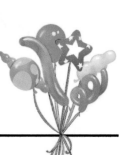

Finger Snacks

You will need

bowl   4 cups boiling water   spoon   eggbeater

2 large boxes   pan   knife
flavored gelatin

1. ⚠️ **Hot** Put all the gelatin in a bowl. Your teacher will add the hot water.

2. Stir until all the gelatin dissolves.

3. Beat the mixture with an eggbeater.

4. Pour the mixture into a pan. Chill it in the refrigerator.

5. Use a knife to cut it into small squares.

Wheels and Axles and Ramps

The carnival is over!
Everyone helps put things away.

The boy pulls his wagon.
It moves on wheels and axles.

The girls push a box up a ramp.

Wheels and axles and ramps are called simple machines. These machines make work easier.

Moving Along

You will need

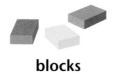
blocks

long board

car

1. Use blocks. Build some steps.

2. Take turns. Push and pull a toy car up the steps.

3. Use boards. Build a ramp.

4. Take turns. Push and pull a toy car up the ramp. Which is easier? Why?

Meet a Mechanic!

Bob Kotter is my name. I work as a mechanic in an auto shop. I use many tools and machines to help me fix cars. The work I do makes cars run better. It also makes cars safer to drive.

At times, a car needs a new battery or new tires. Other times, the oil must be changed. Used oil, tires, and batteries can pollute the environment. Mechanics follow special rules to recycle these things.

Glossary

force *page D7*
A push or a pull.

gravity *page D12*
A force that pulls things toward the center of the earth.

machine *page D18*
A tool that makes our work easier.

magnet *page D14*
A piece of metal that can attract, or draw to it, iron or steel.

ramp *page D20*
A slanting surface that connects different levels.

wheel and axle *page D20*
A wheel with a rod through the center.

CONSTRUCTION SITE

Rocks, Sand, Soil

CONSTRUCTION SITE

Contents

Everybody Needs a Rock

by Byrd Baylor

Everybody
needs
a rock.

I'm sorry for kids
who don't have
a rock
for a friend.

I'm sorry for kids
who only have
TRICYCLES
BICYCLES
HORSES
ELEPHANTS
GOLDFISH
THREE-ROOM PLAYHOUSES
FIRE ENGINES
WIND-UP DRAGONS
AND THINGS LIKE THAT—

if
they don't have
a
rock
for a friend.

Rocks All Around

The earth is made of many kinds of rocks.
Rocks are found everywhere.
Some rocks are on top of the ground.
Other rocks are under the ground
and on the bottom of oceans and streams.

Some rocks are rough.
Other rocks are smooth.

Some rocks are shiny.
Other rocks are dull.

Some rocks are very hard.
Other rocks are soft and
crumbly.

Study a Rock

You will need

rock

hand lens

Activity
Journal
48

recording
sheet

crayons

1. Use a hand lens. Look carefully at your rock.

2. Draw a picture of your rock. Color the picture to match the rock.

3. Tell about your rock. Tell about its size, color, and shape. Tell about how it feels.

More About Rocks

Rocks come in different sizes, colors, and shapes.

Grouping Rocks

You will need

rocks   hand lens   butcher paper

Gypsum

Shale

1. Look at all the rocks to see how they are alike and different. Then sort the rocks into groups.

Flint

Limestone

Pumice

Obsidian

Granite

2. Think of words that tell how you grouped the rocks.

3. Write the words at the top of the butcher paper. Draw lines to make a graph.

4. Put the rocks on the graph where they belong.

5. Tell about the graph.

Marble

Slate

Schist

Changing Rocks

Rocks are always changing.
Large rocks become small.
Small rocks become even smaller.
Many things can cause changes in rocks.

A fast river made this deep canyon.

Bits of rock blown by the wind can change rocks.

Icy glaciers carry and break rocks.

Rock-and-Roll Rocks

You will need

rocks

hand lens

tub with lid

filter paper

water

rubber band

plastic cup

1. Use a hand lens to look at the rocks.

2. Put your rocks into a tub. Fasten the lid with a rubber band. Shake the tub hard for five minutes.

3. Take off the lid. Pour water over the rocks. Take them out.

4. Put the filter into the cup. Pour the water through the filter into the cup.

5. Look at the filter and the rocks with a hand lens. What do you see?

Roots can split rocks.

This building is being cleaned because chemicals in the air changed the color of the bricks.

All About Sand

Sand is made from rocks.
Wind, water, and ice break
rocks into tiny pieces.
The tiny pieces of sand are
called grains.

What can you do with sand?

Exploring Sand

You will need

 spoon   straw   cups and molds   sand   water   hand lens

First, try each step with dry sand.

1. Run your hands through the sand. How does it feel?

2. Stir the sand with a spoon. What happens to the grains?

3. Gently blow the sand with a straw. How do the grains move?

4. Pack sand in cups and molds. Turn them over. What happens?

Now, make the sand wet. Do each step again.

Rocks and Sand

People use rocks and sand in many ways.

Shale and limestone are used to make bricks.

Basalt is crushed to make gravel.

Slate is split to make roof tiles.

Granite rocks are piled to make a wall.

Sand is melted to make glass.

Designs in Sand

You will need

sand paint powders spoon cardboard glue and brush

1. Mix different colors of paint powder in each cup of sand.

2. Use a pencil to draw a picture on the cardboard.

3. Brush glue on one part of the picture at a time.

4. Sprinkle sand on the wet glue. Use one color at a time.

5. Tap the picture to shake off extra sand.

Spotlight on Soil

Soil is made of tiny pieces
of rock, sand, or clay.
Soil has bits of living things
that have died.
Insects, worms, and other animals
live in soil.
Plants grow in soil.

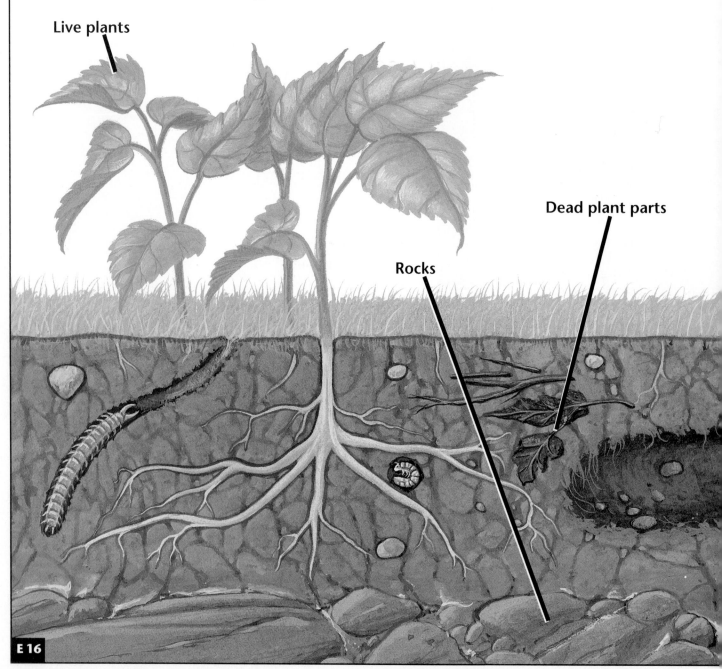

Live plants

Dead plant parts

Rocks

Close-Up on Soil

You will need

hand lens

crayons

plates

3 kinds of soil

Activity Journal 50
recording sheet

1. Put each soil sample on a different plate.

2. Look at each kind of soil with a hand lens. Touch the soil and smell it.

3. Spread out the dark soil. Sort the things you find in it.

4. Draw and label the things you find.

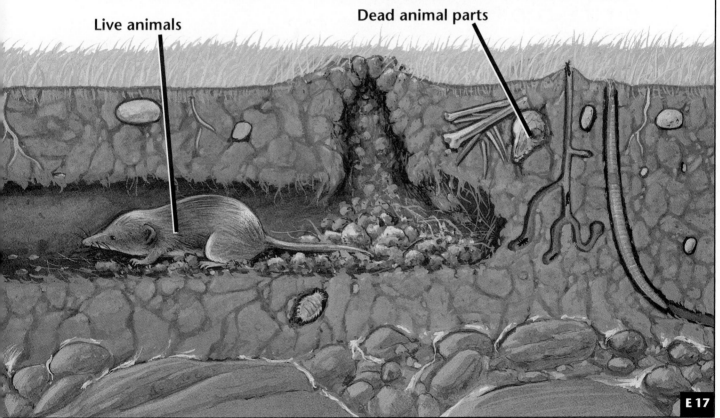

Live animals

Dead animal parts

E 17

A Closer Look at Soil

Many living things need soil.
Soil holds water that plants
and animals need. Soil has air that
living things need, too.

How can you show that soil holds air?

Soil Secrets

You will need

cups   crayon   soil   water   recording sheet

1. Put soil in a cup. Draw a line
on the cup to show the
top of the soil.

2. Use your fingers. Pack down the soil. What happens to the soil? Draw a line on the cup to show the new soil line.

3. Show the two soil lines on your paper. Tell what you think happened.

4. Fill another cup with soil. Add water to the cup. What do you see? What do you think happened?

Uses of Soil

Soil has many uses.
People use soil in different ways.
Animals use soil in different ways, too.

Animals often find food in soil.

Soil is used to grow flowers and trees.

Soil is used for growing food.

Robins use damp soil or mud to build nests. How does mud hold a nest together?

The Best Nest

You will need

cardboard

dry grass, mud, leaves and twigs

art supplies

Activity Journal 52

recording sheet

1. Look at the dry grass, mud, leaves, and twigs. Choose what you will use to build a nest.

2. Plan your nest. Draw it on your paper.

3. Make a nest. Build it on the cardboard.

4. Write about your nest.

Many animals use soil to build nests and dens.

Meet a Contractor!

Hi! I'm Joycelyn Thompson. I am a building contractor. My crew and I work together to build houses, apartments, and stores. We work from special plans called blueprints. These plans must follow all the building laws of the town.

CONSTRUCTION SITE • Rocks, Sand, Soil • Careers and Environment

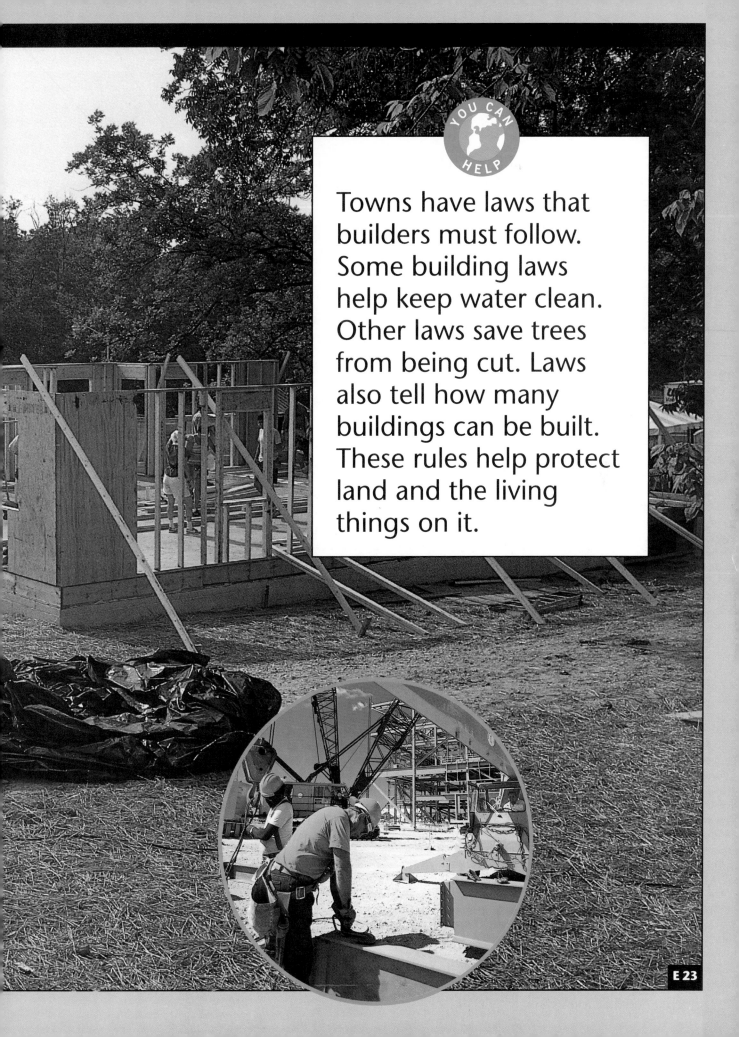

Towns have laws that builders must follow. Some building laws help keep water clean. Other laws save trees from being cut. Laws also tell how many buildings can be built. These rules help protect land and the living things on it.

Glossary

brick *page E14*
A block made of clay that is baked by fire or the sun.

clay *page E16*
A type of earth that can be shaped when wet and hardens when it is baked or dried.

gravel *page E14*
Rock pieces and small stones used for paving roads and paths.

rock *page E6*
A hard material made up of minerals.

sand *page E12*
Tiny bits or grains of broken rock.

soil *page E16*
Earth or dirt made of rock and pieces of living things that have died.

BEACH

Weather and Seasons

BEACH

Contents

Rain Talk

By Mary Serfozo

Ploomp go the first fat raindrops,
Ploomp Ploomp Ploomp
into the soft summer dust
of a country road.
Each little drop digs a dark little hole
and the smell of wet dust tickles my nose.

On the old tin roof of the garden shed
the drops all try to talk at once...
Ping Ping PingaDing
Ping Ping Ping Ping Ping...
and they chuckle together
as they run down the drain.

It's raining harder now.
Listen to the
PlipPlipPlipPlipPlipPlip
as it speckles the smooth surface of the pond.
To Mother Duck
that says, "Time to go for a swim."

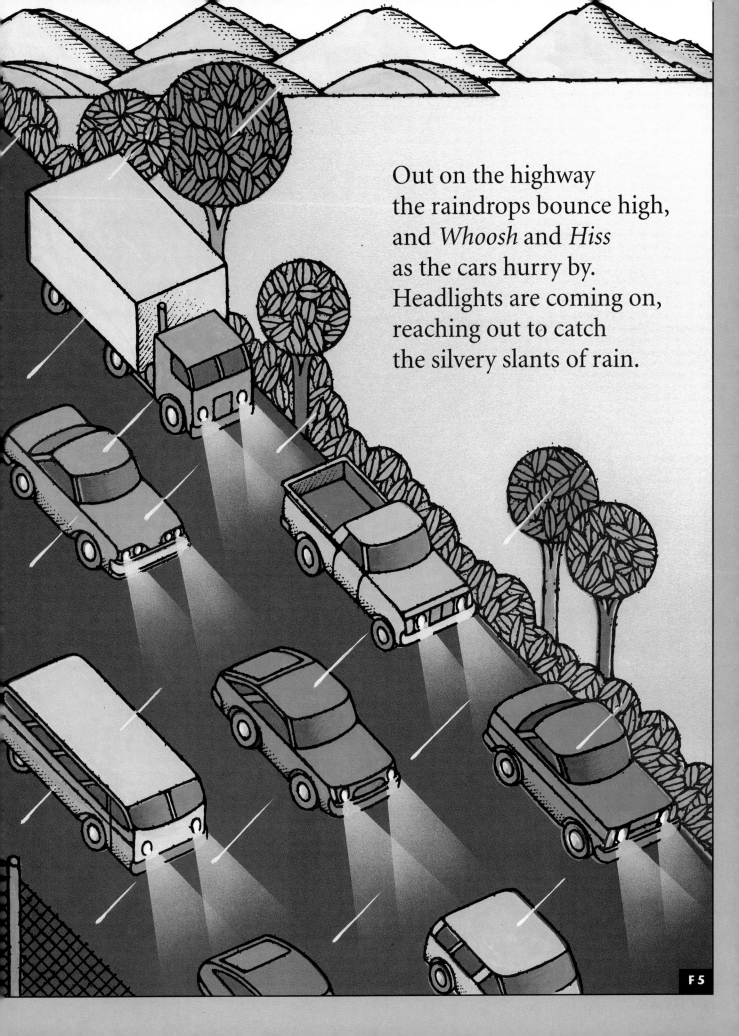

Out on the highway
the raindrops bounce high,
and *Whoosh* and *Hiss*
as the cars hurry by.
Headlights are coming on,
reaching out to catch
the silvery slants of rain.

Sunny Days

The sun warms the earth.

BEACH • Weather and Seasons • Lesson 1

A thermometer measures temperature.

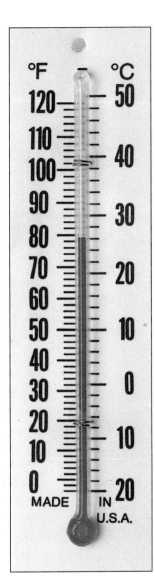

Measuring Air Temperature

You will need

red crayon

thermometer

Activity Journal 59

recording sheet

1. Put a 🌡 in a shady spot.

2. Look at the 🌡 in the morning. Where is the top of the red line?

3. Color a matching line on the first 🌡 on your paper. Write the time under your 🌡 .

4. Do this again around noon and later in the afternoon.

5. Compare the three 🌡 . Tell what happened to the temperature.

Windy Days

Wind is moving air.
Wind can move things.

Wind can be helpful.

The wind moves a sailboat.

The wind turns a windmill.

Wind can be harmful.

The wind knocks down trees.

How strong is the wind?

Making a Pinwheel

You will need

pushpin   art supplies   pattern   unsharpened pencil with eraser

Activity Journal 61

1. Paste the pinwheel pattern onto paper. Cut on the lines.

2. Bring each corner with an X to the center. Use tape to hold the corners.

3. ⚠ **Sharp** Push a pin through the center of the pinwheel. Then push the pin into an eraser.

4. Take your pinwheel outside. Watch it spin. Is it fast or slow? What does it tell you about the wind?

About Clouds

Clouds form from water vapor in the air. They form when the air gets cool.

Clouds are made up of tiny drops of water or ice.

Some clouds are dark and puffy. They may bring heavy rains, lightning, and thunder.

Some clouds are tall, white, and puffy. They look like cotton balls.

Sometimes clouds are near the ground. These clouds are called fog.

Some clouds are high and thin. They look like feathers.

Cloud Watching

You will need

 cup

 hot water

black paper

 flashlight

1. **Hot** Have your teacher pour hot water into a cup.

2. Hold black paper behind the cup.

3. Shine a flashlight through the cloud. See the tiny water drops. You're watching a cloud.

Spring at the Beach

In spring, the days grow longer.
The air gets warmer.
In some places, the weather is rainy.

Birds build nests and lay eggs.
Many new animals are born.
Plants and trees begin to bud.

A Bouquet of Buds

You will need

branch with buds   hand lens   plastic bottle   Activity Journal 67 — recording sheet

1. Put the branch in water.

2. Keep it in a warm, bright place.

3. Look at the buds each day. See how they change.

4. Keep a record. Draw a picture showing what happens to the buds each day.

In summer, days are longer.
The air is often hot.

Young birds and animals grow bigger.
They learn to care for themselves.
Plants and trees have leaves.
Many flowers bloom.
Fruits and other crops grow.

Flitting Butterflies

You will need

construction paper scissors pattern tape straw

Activity Journal 68

1. Cut out the butterfly wings and body.

2. Put the body between the wings. Tape the wings to the body.

3. Tape the body to a straw.

4. Move the butterfly up and down to flap the wings.

In autumn, the days are shorter. The air is crisp and cool.

The young birds and animals are now grown up. Some birds fly south. Many animals store food. Some trees have brightly colored leaves. These leaves then drop. Crops are ready to pick.

Autumn Touch Board

You will need

leaves and seeds   nuts   cardboard   white glue   jar lid

1. Draw six circles on a piece of cardboard.

2. Choose plants, seeds, nuts, and other things that remind you of autumn.

3. Glue an autumn thing in each circle.

4. Gently touch the different circles. Tell what autumn feels like to you.

In winter, days are short.
The air becomes colder.
In some places, the ground
is covered with snow.

Some animals eat the food
they stored in autumn.
Other animals sleep.
Many trees have bare branches.
Some plants die.

Snowflake Mobile

You will need:

paper squares   scissors   hanger   string   tape

1. Fold a square like this.

2. Fold it in half again.

3. Then fold the paper in 3 parts. Cut off the top.

4. Keep the paper folded. Cut out shapes on the fold lines. Then open the paper.

5. Make 3 more snowflakes.

6. Tape a string to each snowflake. Tape the end of each string to a hanger.

Meet a Weather Forecaster!

My name is Mark McEwen. I am a weather forecaster. My job is to find out what the weather will be like. Will you need a sweater today? Will you need an umbrella? Is it a good day for the beach? My forecasts may help you decide.

Here are some tools that help Mark make his forecast.

A weather balloon measures the air. It shows how warm the air is. It also tells which way the wind is blowing and how fast.

A weather satellite in space takes pictures of the earth. The pictures help Mark tell what the weather will be.

Glossary

cloud *page F10*
A white or dark mass in the sky made up of tiny drops of water.

hail *page F13*
Raindrops that freeze and fall to the earth as small, somewhat round bits of ice.

rain *page F10*
Water that falls in drops from clouds in the sky.

sleet *page F12*
Rain that becomes partly frozen when it passes through cold air as it falls to the earth.

snow *page F13*
Water vapor that freezes, forms clouds of frozen crystals, and falls to the earth as white flakes.

temperature *page F7*
How hot or cold something is.

water vapor *page F10*
The name given to water when it is a gas.

wind *page F8*
Moving air.